I went to the Zoo in my tutu!

by Kim and Steve Henderson

Illustrated by Molly Cherry

Dedication

To Kopelynn and Madilynn Jane, With Love

My clothes are washing . . .

What can I wear?

I want to go see the lions and bears!

Aunt Kim is waiting.

What do I do?

I'll put on my favorite blue tutu!

The gate at the front read,

Welcome to the Zoo!

TICKETS

The lady in the booth said,
"My, my! What a pretty tutu!"

First, we see monkeys
swinging from tree to tree.

They shook the branches

and

showered me with leaves.

We see tall giraffes munching leaves from the trees.

And bears licking honey, swarmed by buzzing bees.

Aunt Kim said,

"Oh Koko, what a beautiful view!"

Then she gave me a hug in my pretty blue tutu.

ROAR!

When the lion roared, I just knew,
He was saying how much he loved me in my pretty blue tutu.

We see a peacock, so bright and so blue,
Its feathers as blue as my fluffy tutu!

My tutu got a sniff from an elephant's trunk

And got splashed by a big hippo's dunk.

Next, we see a kangaroo,

hopping so high and so true.

I can hop as high as a kangaroo
in my favorite tutu.

"For lunch," says Aunt Kim, "let's have ice cream!
I love it, and I know you will too."

So for lunch, I ate a scoop that matched my pretty tutu.

Next at the zoo, we see a cockatoo!
He squawked at me in my - you guessed it! - blue tutu.

When we saw the owls, I just knew,
They were saying,

"Who, who,
is the pretty girl in the blue
tutu?

At the petting zoo, I got to feed a goat and an ewe.

I felt a tug and saw it chew, chew a hole in
my favorite tutu!

I watched a flock of penguins playing on the ice.

Then the seals barked at me and splashed me twice.

When we circled the zoo, we were almost through.
A baby chimp yawned, and I did too.

Aunt Kim smiled, our day was fun.

Time for my jammies, my tutu is done!

The best part of going to the zoo,

Was wearing my pretty tutu and exploring it with you!

To our great-niece Koko,
the inspiration behind this book.

Love, Aunt Kim and Uncle Steve

Printed in the USA
CPSIA information can be obtained
at www.ICGtesting.com
LVHW060327060124
768271LV00002B/30